MW01675429

Original title:

Intimacy Innovations

Author: Paulina Pähkel

ISBN HARDBACK: 978-9916-89-154-4

ISBN PAPERBACK: 978-9916-89-155-1

ISBN EBOOK: 978-9916-89-156-8

Affection in Augmented Reality

In a world where pixels bloom,
Hearts connect beyond the gloom.
Virtual whispers fill the air,
Love transcends with each shared stare.

Holograms dance in soft light's glow,
Hands reach out, worlds overflow.
In this realm, emotions play,
Boundless love finds its own way.

Every glance a vibrant spark,
Guiding souls through the dark.
Augmented dreams weave tight and near,
Crafting love without a fear.

Nuances of Proximity

In every step, a heartbeat speaks,
The distance shrinks as silence peaks.
Eyes lock softly, breaths align,
In this space, your warmth is mine.

Words unspoken tell the tale,
Of closeness where we shall not fail.
Each moment shared, a treasure found,
In nuances, our hearts are bound.

Heartbeat echoes in the air,
In proximity, we lay bare.
A gentle touch, a knowing glance,
In this dance, we take a chance.

The Language of Soft Screens

Fingers glide on glass so sleek,
Messages form without a speak.
In silent tones, we find our way,
A language built of night and day.

Emojis paint emotions bright,
Each swipe ignites a spark of light.
In virtual realms, our voices soar,
Together here, we seek for more.

Words appear, a colorful stream,
In every text, a whispered dream.
Soft screens hold what hearts convey,
Love wraps us in this gentle sway.

Beyond the Touchscreen

In realms unseen, connections grow,
Beyond touchscreens, love does flow.
Feelings leap against the tide,
In the shadows, we confide.

As pixels fade, our souls ignite,
In the vastness of the night.
Though screens may separate us here,
In spirit's grasp, we draw near.

Every click, a path we carve,
A journey bold where hearts can starve.
Yet in that void, a bond remains,
Love unyielding, free from chains.

Whispers of Connection

In the silent night we share,
Soft glances spark a tale,
Hearts echo in the still air,
Together, we set sail.

Words left unspoken linger,
Between the beats of time,
Each heartbeat feels like a singer,
In rhythm, pure and sublime.

Through laughter and silent tears,
Threads weaving our design,
The closeness erases fears,
Two souls forever entwined.

A Tapestry of Touch

Fingers dance upon the skin,
A gentle brush, a spark ignites,
Every caress tells where we've been,
In shadows, love ignites.

With every stroke, a story flows,
Each heartbeat finds its place,
In the depth, our essence grows,
Entranced in soft embrace.

Woven in the fabric grand,
Moments meet and intertwine,
Crafted by unseen hands,
In silence, we define.

The Art of Quiet Knowing

In stillness, thoughts collide,
A knowing glance ignites the spark,
In silence, we confide,
Finding light within the dark.

The unspoken language flows,
Through every lingering breath,
In depths where wisdom grows,
Connecting life and death.

In the calm, the truth reveals,
A bond that time won’t sever,
In the heart, the spirit heals,
Together, now and forever.

Secrets Underneath Skin

Soft secrets ride the breeze,
Whispers tucked away from light,
In hidden places, sweet unease,
Yearning for the night.

Touched by shadows, dreams ignite,
Silent pacts of trust we keep,
In a world where hearts take flight,
Awake while others sleep.

Beneath the surface, stories lie,
In layers thick with time,
In tender moments, we can fly,
To where love’s bells chime.

Gentle Radiance

Soft whispers kiss the dawn,
Golden light begins to play.
Nature's canvas stretches wide,
Awakening a brand new day.

Petals glisten, dew like pearls,
Breezes dance through bending grass.
Every moment sings of hope,
In this fragile morn, we pass.

Clouds drift gently overhead,
Sunlight breaks through every seam.
With a warmth that soothes the heart,
Life unfolds just like a dream.

Quiet thoughts, the world in pause,
Each ray treasures what is near.
Hands brush lightly, souls entwined,
In this glow, we find our clear.

Echoing in silent woods,
Nature hums its sweet refrain.
In the hush, we find our peace,
Gentle radiance, love's sustain.

The Alchemy of Two

Together we forge a path,
Hearts entwined in laughter's light.
Every glance ignites a spark,
In your presence, all feels right.

Words like gold from lips of honey,
Minds connected, softly bound.
In the chaos, you are calm,
In your stillness, joy is found.

Two lives dance in sweet embrace,
Twirling under moonlit skies.
Hands entwined, we share our dreams,
In this alchemy, we rise.

Moments fleeting, yet so vast,
We weave memories, thread by thread.
In this tapestry of love,
Together, we are gently led.

With each heartbeat, stronger still,
Our spirits blend and intertwine.
You and I, a perfect pair,
In the alchemy, we shine.

In the Fold of Warmth

Crimson embers, softly glow,
Sparks of comfort fill the room.
Wrapped within each other's arms,
In our haven, love will bloom.

Whispers linger, secrets shared,
Like a blanket, soft and wide.
In the fold of warmth we bask,
Joy and solace, side by side.

The world outside can wait its turn,
Here, the worries fade away.
In our cocoon, time is still,
In this moment, we shall stay.

Every sigh a melody,
As the night enfolds the day.
Hearts in rhythm, pulse in sync,
In warmth's embrace, we find our way.

Stars above, bright witness to,
The bond we tightly keep alive.
In the fold of warmth, we learn,
Together always, we will thrive.

Mapping Uncharted Bonds

Hand in hand, we chart the course,
Through the wild, untouched terrain.
With each step, we trace the lines,
In the silence, love's refrain.

Hearts united, spirits free,
Exploring depths of trust anew.
In every glance, a promise forms,
Mapping paths that lead to you.

Together we cross rivers wide,
Scaling heights, we find our way.
Every challenge strengthens ties,
In this journey, come what may.

Moments dance like flickering stars,
Guiding us through night’s embrace.
In this uncharted territory,
Together we have found our place.

With each heartbeat, trails unfold,
Every memory guides our flight.
In the mapping of our bonds,
We create a love that's bright.

The Fabric of Feeling

Threads of joy weave through the days,
Colors bright in sunlit rays,
Whispers softly stitch the night,
Emotions dance in pure delight.

Laughter quilted in our hearts,
Stitched together, never parts,
Gentle sorrow finds a seam,
Layered depth in every dream.

Patterns formed from love and care,
Intertwined in moments rare,
Woven tight, yet free we roam,
In this fabric, we find home.

Each patch holds a story told,
In vibrant hues of green and gold,
We wear our hearts like woven art,
The threads connect, never depart.

In silence shared, our fates align,
A tapestry, your hand in mine,
As we create this sacred space,
The fabric of feeling, our embrace.

Poetic Proximity

Words like notes in evening air,
Close enough to feel the flare,
Rhythms whisper, hearts in tune,
In their glow, we find our boon.

Lines entwine, like fingers clasped,
Close together, moments grasped,
Breath in sync beneath the stars,
Poetic proximity, no bars.

Silent verses, gaze and pause,
In this dance, we find our cause,
Every glance, a stanza made,
Every heartbeat, gently played.

Between the words, the spaces lie,
Where meanings swirl and softly sigh,
In the closeness, poetry grows,
From the intimacy, beauty flows.

We etch our verses in the night,
Together casting shadows bright,
In the ebb and flow we find,
Proximity breeds a loving mind.

Heartbeats in the Night

Softly pulsing in the dark,
Each heartbeat, a whispered spark,
Together lost in quiet dreams,
A rhythm flows, or so it seems.

Moonlit paths we tread so slow,
With every beat, the feelings grow,
In the hush, our secrets share,
Captured moments filled with care.

Echoes linger in the space,
Silent vows interlace with grace,
Close your eyes, let worries drift,
In the night, our spirits lift.

Through shadows cast by silver light,
Heartbeat's song keeps us upright,
In this dance, a tender touch,
The night embraces us so much.

So let the stars our witness be,
As heartbeats blend in harmony,
In the calm where dreams take flight,
We find our solace in the night.

Mutual Reflection

In your eyes, I see my soul,
Mirrored depths, a sacred role,
Every glance, a truth unfolds,
In this bond, our hearts are gold.

Fragments of us intertwine,
Reflections of the divine,
Shared whispers, thoughts collide,
In our gaze, we cannot hide.

Gentle ripples on the lake,
Pulse of trust, the heart awake,
With every look, a story spun,
In our sphere, we are as one.

Through the storms and sunny days,
In our mirrors, love's bright rays,
Mutual growth, a dance we share,
In this space, we're free to dare.

So let the world fade away,
In this moment, here we stay,
True reflections, side by side,
In our hearts, the love abides.

The Language of Fingertips

Whispers soft upon the skin,
Touching words where love begins.
Fingers trace the hidden lines,
In the silence, heart defines.

Every brush, a tale to tell,
Like a secret, cast a spell.
In the dance of flesh and bone,
Fingertips speak what's not shown.

Gentle pressure, sweet caress,
Through the touch, we feel our best.
In the warmth, the truth we find,
Mapping dreams, so intertwined.

Moments shared in quiet grace,
Each connection leaves a trace.
In the language of the night,
Fingertips weave our shared light.

When the world fades out of sight,
In your touch, I find my light.
Every heartbeat, pulse, and sigh,
In this language, we can fly.

Closeness Redefined

In a world that pulls apart,
We redefine the beating heart.
Side by side, our spirits blend,
In the warmth, we learn to mend.

Words unspoken share the glow,
In the stillness, love will grow.
Though distance may try to sever,
In our bond, we're strong forever.

Hours spent in quiet grace,
Every smile a warm embrace.
In the moments, time stands still,
Hand in hand, we bend our will.

Echoes of a soft refrain,
In our closeness, joy and pain.
Through the trials, we remain,
Redefined, we break the chain.

As the stars light up the sky,
In your gaze, I learn to fly.
With each heartbeat, trust reclaims,
In this closeness, love names.

A Dance of Shadows

Underneath the silver moon,
Whispers weave an ancient tune.
Dancing softly, night's embrace,
In the shadows, we find grace.

Every flicker tells a tale,
Shapes entwine where dreams prevail.
In the dark, the spirits sway,
Moving gently, night to day.

Echoed laughter fills the air,
Through the silence, we both share.
Our reflections twist and twine,
In the shadows, hearts align.

With each step, the world confides,
In the dance where hope resides.
Lost in rhythm, lost in time,
In this waltz, our souls will climb.

As the dawn begins to break,
In the light, we softly wake.
Shadows fade, but not the feel,
In this dance, our hearts reveal.

Spectrum of Us

Colors blend in vibrant hues,
Every shade a tale to choose.
In the spectrum, life unfolds,
Painting stories yet untold.

You are blue, the deep and vast,
In your calm, I've found my past.
I'm the red that burns so bright,
Together, we ignite the night.

Golden rays that touch the soul,
In your warmth, I feel more whole.
With each shade, we weave the scene,
In this canvas, hearts convene.

Tints of green, a soothing balm,
In our laughter, life's a psalm.
Let the colors intertwine,
In our blend, the stars align.

Spectrum wide, a vibrant play,
In your love, I find my way.
Through the shades, forever trust,
In this journey, it's just us.

Heartstrings in the Cloud

In the soft embrace of the sky,
Whispers of love flutter high.
Dreams weave through digital glow,
Heartstrings pulse in the flow.

Through pixels, we share our thoughts,
In the ether, the heart's knots.
Each heart emoji, a gentle nudge,
A virtual touch, a tender bud.

Clouds may hide our shared spaces,
Yet in dreams, we find our traces.
Distance fades in the light of screens,
We bridge the gap with hopes and dreams.

Beneath the stars, we start to dance,
Woven together in our romance.
Though miles apart, our spirits soar,
Love's melody forevermore.

So here's to hearts, both near and far,
Connected by wishes beneath the stars.
In the cloud, our stories blend,
With each heartbeat, we transcend.

Rebel Affection

In a world that says we must fight,
Our hearts are rebels, taking flight.
With starlit eyes, we break the mold,
In whispered dreams, our love unfolds.

Chasing shadows through the night,
Defying odds, igniting light.
You and I, we dance to chance,
In every glance, a bold romance.

No rules to bind, no chains to sway,
In our hearts, love finds its way.
Hand in hand, we stand the test,
Through storms and trials, we are blessed.

To live our truth, we'll take a stand,
With fire and grit, we know we can.
Emotions blaze like a raging sea,
In our rebellion, we are free.

Together, we'll paint the skies,
With vibrant hues and daring ties.
Rebel affection, wild and true,
In every heartbeat, it's me and you.

Emotions Encoded

In silent texts and coded dreams,
Feelings dance in digital streams.
Between the lines, our hearts lay bare,
Encoded messages fill the air.

With every click, you see my soul,
A language shared, we are made whole.
In binary beats, our passions hum,
Emotions coded, love's sweet drum.

Through mists of pixels, love ignites,
Fleeting glimpses of cherished sights.
Heartfelt shades, in colors bright,
We navigate this endless night.

Though screens may blur what’s felt inside,
In whispers soft, we will confide.
A tapestry of hearts entwined,
In every byte, our love defined.

So let our hearts in silence speak,
With every pulse, together seek.
Emotions encoded, clear as day,
In this vast world, you light my way.

Choreography of Distance

In the dance of stars, we twirl,
Two souls apart, yet love will swirl.
Each step we take, a measured grace,
In this vast space, we find our place.

With every heartbeat, a rhythm beats,
In the waltz of life, our love repeats.
Through distant dreams, we move as one,
A choreography beneath the sun.

Though miles may separate our touch,
In heart's ballet, we yearn so much.
Every tear, a note we play,
In silent songs, love finds its way.

In twilight’s glow, we share our plight,
With every breath, we fight the night.
Two hearts aligned in perfect time,
In distance, we find our love's rhyme.

So here we stand, though far apart,
Two dancers with a single heart.
In the choreography of our dreams,
Love transcends all, or so it seems.

Whispers in the Dark

In shadows deep, secrets dwell,
Softly speaking, tales to tell.
Stars above, a silent spark,
Embracing dreams, whispers in the dark.

Quiet moments, hearts align,
Gentle echoes, love's design.
Breath of night, a tender mark,
Forever bound, whispers in the dark.

Moonlit paths, a fleeting gleam,
Holding close, a shared dream.
Fearless souls, ignite the spark,
Together lost, whispers in the dark.

Kaleidoscope of Affection

Colors blend, feelings soar,
A vibrant dance, forevermore.
Shifting hues, a love affair,
In this lens, we find our care.

Fragments bright, captured light,
Every glance, a new delight.
Whirls of joy, shadows part,
In this frame, a beating heart.

Through the glass, we see it clear,
A universe, holding near.
Infinite paths, a work of art,
In your eyes, a kaleidoscope of affection.

Echoes of the Heartbeat

In the night, a rhythm plays,
Soft and steady, love's sweet ways.
A gentle thrum, the world stands still,
In this moment, hearts fulfill.

Between the beats, a silence grows,
A language whispered, only we know.
Time suspends, tears depart,
In the echoes, we find our heart.

Through the storm, through the calm,
Every pulse, an endless balm.
Together bound, never apart,
In the echoes of the heartbeat.

Embraced in Silence

In quiet spaces, love resides,
No words needed, warmth abides.
A gentle touch, a knowing glance,
In stillness, we find our dance.

Softly shared, the breath of peace,
In this hush, we find release.
Wrapped in arms, we lose the fight,
Embraced in silence, pure delight.

Golden moments, softly spun,
Two souls drifting, become one.
In silence held, hearts take flight,
Together lost, embraced in silence.

Whispered Secrets of Metal and Glass

In the twilight, shadows dance,
Reflections flicker, hold their chance.
Silent whispers, secrets spared,
In every glint, a story shared.

Rusty rivets, dreams of flight,
Fractured glasses catch the light.
A moment captured, frozen time,
Echoed thoughts, a quiet rhyme.

Beneath the surface, stories hide,
In every creak, emotions glide.
The heart of steel, the soul of glass,
In fragile bonds, we find our path.

Tales of ages, forged anew,
In every shard, a glimpse of you.
The beauty found in worn-out seams,
Weaving together, our wildest dreams.

So let the metal sing its song,
In every twist, where we belong.
Glass whispers softly, secrets dear,
In the night, our truth shines clear.

Vows in the Vortex

In swirling currents, two hearts meet,
Promises woven, bittersweet.
Spiraling hopes in the tempest's embrace,
Each vow a star in the endless space.

Whirlwinds curling, time entwined,
In every gust, our fates aligned.
Through chaos we dance, blissfully lost,
In the eye of the storm, we bear the cost.

A vortex of passion, we'll brave the night,
With whispered dreams that take their flight.
Through trials deep, we'll stand as one,
Bound by the bond that can't be undone.

Kisses like lightning, fierce and bright,
In the maelstrom, we find our light.
Together we'll spin, forever we'll vow,
In the heart of the vortex, we live here and now.

Through the whirl, love's grace will steer,
In every storm, I'll hold you near.
Wrapped in wonder, fiercely entwined,
In the swirling dance, our souls aligned.

Radiant Synapses

Neurons sparking, bright and bold,
Whispers of thoughts yet to unfold.
Connections buzzing, electric glee,
In brilliant patterns, we roam free.

Synaptic treasures, infinite minds,
In every thought, the universe finds.
Cosmic light in brain’s embrace,
Each glow a memory, time and space.

Connect the dots, ignite the flame,
In this dance of thought, we play the game.
Ideas collide, a vibrant thread,
In every insight, the past is fed.

Colors merging, vividly bright,
Eureka moments, a pure delight.
Within the spark, a world ignites,
As radiant synapses reach new heights.

Together we journey, explore each strand,
In the realm of knowledge, hand in hand.
With every flash, the cosmos sings,
In radiant wonder, new life springs.

Threads of Light and Love

In gentle weavings, moments gleam,
Threads of joy, a shared dream.
Fingers entwined, soft and tight,
In the fabric of time, we find our light.

Each golden strand, a story spun,
In laughter's echo, we become one.
With every stitch, love's embrace,
In tender warmth, we find our place.

Woven patterns of hope arise,
In the tapestry, a sweet surprise.
Sunset hues in every thread,
Binding our hearts, where we are led.

Through trials faced, the fabric bends,
Yet love survives and never ends.
A quilt of memories, soft and true,
In every thread, there's me and you.

So let us weave with colors bright,
In the threads of love, our hearts take flight.
With every moment stitched with care,
Together we rise, a bond so rare.

Echoing Embraces

In twilight's gentle grip, we stay,
Soft whispers dance in the fading day.
Your heartbeat syncs with mine in the night,
Together, we fill the dark with light.

Each moment shared, a silent tone,
Echoing love in spaces unknown.
With every glance, our spirits bind,
In tender silence, our hearts aligned.

The world fades away, just we two,
Wrapped in shadows, a love that's true.
In these echoes, our dreams arise,
In the night, under starlit skies.

Your laughter's song in the breeze,
A melody that sets me at ease.
We sway to the rhythm, hearts embraced,
In this echo, our love is traced.

A dance of souls in twilight's dusk,
Each moment together, a cherished husk.
In echoes of love, we find our way,
Forever entwined, come what may.

Signals of Togetherness

In the morning light, we rise as one,
Two hearts beating, a journey begun.
Fingers entwined, we walk down the lane,
Each step shared, a lovely refrain.

Your smile, a beacon, shining bright,
Guiding me through the depths of night.
With every laugh, a bond we weave,
In signals of love, we both believe.

The world may shift, but we stay true,
Our hearts echo, always anew.
In each whisper, a promise sings,
Together we soar on love's pure wings.

Through seasons that change and time that flows,
In the garden of us, resilience grows.
We harvest joy, we cherish pain,
In signals of togetherness, we gain.

So let the stars guide our way,
In every night, in every day.
Our love a language, simple and sweet,
In signals of togetherness, we meet.

Stories Beneath the Screen

In the glow of light, our stories unfold,
Words tapping soft, a truth to be told.
Underneath the screen, a world of dreams,
Life intertwines in delicate seams.

Each message sent, a moment shared,
In digital realms, our souls are bared.
Pixels dance, emotions collide,
In stories beneath, our hearts confide.

Late-night whispers, laughter that glows,
Through glowing screens, affection grows.
In every click, a connection sings,
A tapestry woven with invisible strings.

Yet in the silence, we seek the real,
Beneath the surface, a deeper feel.
Together we wander, hand in hand,
Discovering treasures, in this land.

So here's to the nights of shared dreams,
And stories that flow like gentle streams.
In the depths of the screen, love's light beams,
Creating a bond richer than it seems.

Unveiling Layers of Us

Beneath the surface, whispers abide,
In each shared moment, we confide.
Layers reveal in the quiet night,
Unveiling our souls, in soft daylight.

With tender eyes, we peel away,
The masks we wear in the light of day.
Vulnerability blooms, a radiant sight,
In the garden of trust, we ignite.

Each story told, a thread of gold,
Binding our hearts, steadfast and bold.
Through trials and triumphs, hand in hand,
We uncover depths, together we stand.

In the dance of dreams, we find our place,
Unveiling layers with every embrace.
As the world outside softly fades,
In the depths of us, love cascades.

So let us dive into this embrace,
Exploring the depths, the sacred space.
In layers unveiled, our hearts interlace,
Creating a tapestry, time can't erase.

Intimate Horizons of Technology

In glowing screens our secrets lie,
Holding dreams and whispers shy.
With every tap, a world unveiled,
Connections forged, yet hearts impaled.

Pixels dance in a neon haze,
Minutes blend into digital days.
Bytes of love, in silence they swell,
Echoes of feelings, hard to tell.

We reach across virtual space,
Finding solace in data's embrace.
Yet in the maze, shadows creep,
A longing that keeps us from sleep.

In coded hearts, a warmth ignites,
As thoughts collide in endless flights.
Navigating through the virtual mist,
We seek the truths that once we missed.

So let us dream of a day untold,
Where human touch is bravely bold.
In intimate realms, let's find our way,
Through technology's light, come what may.

Soundwaves of Desire

In silence echoes a soft refrain,
Whispers of longing, pleasure and pain.
Each heartbeat syncs with a distant sound,
As souls entwine, a rhythm profound.

Melodies linger in twilight's glow,
Drawing us closer, ebbing like flow.
With every note, emotions collide,
A dance of longing we can't hide.

Songs of the heart in waves of night,
Resonating softly, igniting the light.
Every glance like a gentle caress,
In the symphony, we find our rest.

Cadences weave through shadows and dreams,
Creating a map of starlit themes.
In the chorus of love, we find our place,
In soundwaves of desire, we lose our pace.

As echoes fade, we still remain,
Bound by the rhythm, through joy and pain.
In harmony's whisper, forever we'll sway,
Together in night, come what may.

Graffiti of the Heart

On crumbling walls, our stories rise,
Colors splash like forgotten cries.
With every stroke, our voices blend,
Tales of love that never end.

In urban jungles, dreams take flight,
Chasing shadows into the night.
Spray-painted hopes, a vivid sea,
Expressions wild, raw, and free.

Layers peeled back, secrets exposed,
In alleyways, the truth is composed.
Strokes of passion, lines of despair,
Each mark a memory hanging in air.

We claim our space with bold designs,
Art that heals, though time often pines.
Through vibrant hues, we find our place,
In the graffiti of the heart, we embrace.

So let your spirit dance on the wall,
Let colors shatter the silence's call.
For in these fragments of love's sweet art,
We leave our legacy, a work of heart.

Navigating the Digital Tides

Surfing waves of binary code,
On currents of thought, we share the load.
With each click, we forge our trails,
In this sea of data, our spirit sails.

From calming shores to tempest's roar,
We seek connection, forevermore.
In chat rooms dim and bright displays,
Our voices echo through endless ways.

Navigating storms of pixel and light,
We stand together, both day and night.
In virtual realms, we find our crew,
Building bridges where once there were few.

As tides draw near, our hearts align,
In shared moments, we intertwine.
For through the screen, we create our ties,
In the deep blue, our spirit flies.

With courage bold, we ride the waves,
Unlocking treasures that love engraves.
Navigating the tides, hand in hand,
In the digital realm, we take our stand.

Flickering Memories

In the stillness of the night,
Old whispers dance in dreams,
Echoes of a distant laugh,
Fading like the moonbeams.

A photograph unfolds,
Time captured in sepia,
Moments we hold dear,
Yet slip through our fingers.

The taste of summer rain,
Children playing in the street,
Each drop a fleeting joy,
In rhythm with heartbeats.

Silent shadows linger,
Beneath the rustling leaves,
Stories in the twilight,
Memories never grieve.

Through the corridors of time,
We chase what's left behind,
In flickering memories,
Our hearts are intertwined.

Love Poems in the Age of Algorithms

In the glow of blue screens,
Two hearts beat as one,
We code our deep desires,
Underneath the digital sun.

With clicks and silent texts,
Love takes on new forms,
Shared algorithms binding,
Against the world's norms.

Patterns play like music,
In every byte and line,
A symphony of connection,
Through codes, the stars align.

Yet still, the heart whispers,
In the noise of binary,
True love can't be computed,
It's more than just a diary.

So we write our own verses,
In a language of the heart,
In this age of algorithms,
It's where all love can start.

Tapestry of Transmissions

Woven threads of silence,
Connect us in the night,
Signals drift like whispers,
Bearing tales of light.

In the static of the air,
Voices blend and fade,
Every pulse a story,
In this intricate charade.

The tapestry we weave,
Is stitched with dreams untold,
In every transmission,
A universe unfolds.

When the world is quiet,
And shadows softly sway,
Each message sent is magic,
In its own unique way.

Together we are woven,
In this endless ballet,
In a tapestry of transmissions,
We find our place to stay.

Envelopes of Emotion

In the folds of paper,
Secrets softly lie,
Ink spills out affection,
Underneath the sky.

Each envelope a journey,
Carried by the breeze,
Words become the vessels,
For hearts that wish to seize.

Tears of joy and longing,
Written in a haste,
In every creased corner,
A sentiment embraced.

Whispers in the twilight,
The night's embrace is close,
Through these envelopes of emotion,
We express what matters most.

Forever we will cherish,
These letters that we send,
In every sealed promise,
Love's echoes never end.

Uncharted Territories of Hearts

In quiet whispers, love is born,
Beyond the maps we've drawn in thorn.
With every pulse, a new frontier,
We wander paths, with hearts sincere.

The constellations of our dreams,
Illuminate the night, it seems.
Each heartbeat charts a mystery,
A vast expanse of history.

Through valleys deep and mountains high,
We chase the echo of the sky.
In every glance, a spark ignites,
Exploring realms of pure delights.

With every tear, a lesson learned,
In silent corners, wisdom earned.
Together we untangle fate,
In uncharted lands, we navigate.

A compass made of love's embrace,
Guides us to the hidden place.
Where every moment feels like art,
As we explore our secret heart.

Serenades in the Silence

The hush of night, a serenade,
Unspoken words that never fade.
In silence deep, our souls align,
A symphony of hearts, divine.

Each quiet breath, a gentle hymn,
Where shadows dance on edges dim.
Through moonlit dreams, our spirits soar,
In tranquil realms, we sing once more.

The stillness holds a sacred space,
Where love's soft echoes find their grace.
A whispered note, a tender sigh,
In silence shared, we do not lie.

The world outside can fade away,
In muted tones, we choose to stay.
Together lost in fate's embrace,
Serenades weave through time and space.

With every pause, the heartbeats swell,
A rhythmic tide that casts a spell.
In whispers soft, we choose to dwell,
In serenades, we find our well.

Postcards from the Network

In pixels bright, our stories shared,
Across the lines, we've always cared.
Each message sent, a piece of heart,
Connections formed, though miles apart.

Through glowing screens, we find our way,
In modern dreams, we learn to play.
A snapshot of the day-to-day,
Postcards sent, in shades of gray.

With every click, a moment caught,
In laughter and the battles fought.
We write our tales, both near and far,
In every byte, we wear a scar.

The world expands, the miles dissolve,
In threads of hope, our lives evolve.
A network spun of joy and tears,
Postcards filled, reflecting years.

Digital hearts in endless flow,
With every voice, new seeds to sow.
In pixels bright, we find our light,
Postcards shared through day and night.

The Glow of Synaptic Connections

In tangled webs of thought and spark,
Where neurons dance and leave their mark.
The glow of mind in vivid hues,
Unfolds the paths we choose to use.

With every thought, a river flows,
In currents deep, our knowledge grows.
A luminous path, weaving through,
The synaptic dance, a spark anew.

Through brainwaves bright, we reach the stars,
In silent whispers, we find who we are.
Each connection made, a story spun,
In light we move, as one, as one.

The glow ignites the darkest night,
In every pulse, we find our light.
Through memories, both near and far,
The synaptic glow shines like a star.

In every thought, we intertwine,
Crafting dreams from threads divine.
In endless dance of thought and grace,
The glow of minds, our saving space.

Heartstrings in Harmony

In silence, we share a glance,
The world fades in this dance.
With every beat, we intertwine,
Two souls merging, pure, divine.

Your laughter rings like soothing chimes,
Guiding me through toughest times.
Through trials faced, we stand so tall,
Together, we'll conquer all.

In whispers soft, our hopes take flight,
With dreams as vast as the night.
Boundless skies reflect our trust,
In love, we will always adjust.

Each moment shared, a melody,
A symphony, just you and me.
Forever wrapped in this embrace,
Our heartstrings twined, a sacred space.

With every note, our spirits rise,
Creating magic, beyond the skies.
In harmony, we find our song,
Together, where we both belong.

Developing Depths of Us

Like rivers carving through the land,
We shape our paths, hand in hand.
Each current whispers ancient tales,
Of love that blooms and never fails.

In shadows cast, our truths unfold,
In gentle words, our stories told.
With every challenge, we grow strong,
Through thick and thin, we both belong.

The layers peel, revealing light,
In shared glances, hearts ignite.
Our roots entwined beneath the ground,
In silence, we lose and then find sound.

From shallow pools to ocean's deep,
In dreams we dare, in love we leap.
Each tide brings strength to our embrace,
In quiet moments, we find grace.

As seasons change, we learn to bend,
Embracing flow, we will transcend.
In time's embrace, we craft, we trust,
Developing depths, in love we must.

Beyond the Surface

The waves may crash, the storms may roar,
Yet in the depths, we seek for more.
With courage rising, hearts in sync,
Together we dive, and never sink.

The beauty lies in what we find,
In hidden depths, our souls aligned.
Each treasure shines, a piece of gold,
A story shared, a truth retold.

Through layers thick, we cut away,
To find the light beneath the gray.
A journey long, yet bold we stand,
In every heartbeat, hand in hand.

The depths we forge, a sacred space,
In vulnerability, we find our place.
Beyond the surface, trust will grow,
In loving depths, our spirits flow.

Together, we'll brave the fiercest tides,
Through darkest nights, love still abides.
In every wave that seeks to pull,
We rise above, our hearts so full.

Threads that Bind

Invisible threads weave through our days,
Connecting hearts in countless ways.
With every laugh, with every tear,
These threads become more bright and clear.

In quiet moments, we feel the pull,
Our shared experiences, powerful.
With every story, every sigh,
We stitch our dreams as they pass by.

Though distance grows, we stand so near,
These threads of love keep us sincere.
Through every storm, through every fight,
We hold on tight, to what feels right.

A tapestry of moments spun,
In threads of gold, our lives are done.
Forever linked, through thick and thin,
Together, we'll always begin.

Each day unfolds, a new design,
In every glance, our fates entwined.
With threads that bind, we'll never part,
In woven dreams, you hold my heart.

Luminescent Moments

In twilight's gentle glow, they dance,
Echoes soft in fleeting trance.
Stars whisper secrets in the night,
Illuminating dreams in flight.

Rustling leaves, a song unfolds,
Golden stories yet untold.
Moments gleam like dew at dawn,
A tapestry of hope reborn.

Laughter lingers in the air,
Fragile joy beyond compare.
Time stands still, a breath embraced,
In these moments, love is chased.

With every heartbeat, colors shift,
In the silence, spirits lift.
Radiance found in each small sigh,
Blessings whispered, never shy.

As day fades into velvet skies,
We find our truth in whispered lies.
Luminescent paths we roam,
In these moments, we feel home.

Fading Lines of Solitude

In shadows deep, a heart resides,
Where silence speaks and time abides.
The empty spaces stretch out wide,
A canvas where lost dreams confide.

Wisps of thoughts like autumn leaves,
Drift away while fortune weaves.
In the echoes of the past,
We question how long this will last.

Memories linger, bittersweet,
Footsteps fade, no soul to greet.
The night's embrace, a ghostly shroud,
In solitude, whispers feel loud.

Yet in the hushed confines of night,
A flicker sparks, a distant light.
Fading lines draw closer still,
In solitude, we learn our will.

For in the silence, truths we find,
Woven deep within the mind.
As shadows melt into the dawn,
The lines may fade, but hope lives on.

Tethered Hearts Unseen

Two souls entwined by fate's own thread,
In unseen bonds, their love is spread.
Invisible ties that pull them near,
Strength in silence, crystal clear.

Through life's storms, they softly sway,
Anchored firm, come what may.
Each gentle touch, a whispered plea,
In their hearts, they hold the key.

Stars align in a cosmic dance,
In each glance, a fleeting chance.
Though apart, their spirits blend,
Tethered hearts that will not bend.

In every challenge, they find grace,
A sacred link, a warm embrace.
Together, even when alone,
In love’s symphony, they have grown.

For even when the world feels vast,
Their tethered hearts will ever last.
Invisible threads that bind them tight,
In the dark, they find their light.

Crafted Caresses

Delicate hands sculpting dreams,
In soft whispers, love redeems.
Each caress, a stroke of art,
Crafted tender as the heart.

Gentle kisses like morning dew,
Eager hearts, forever true.
Every touch, a canvas bare,
In passion's glow, they lay it bare.

Moments linger, sweet and slow,
In crafted caresses, love will grow.
With every heartbeat, sparks ignite,
A dance of shadows in the night.

Embers glowing, warmth fulfilled,\nFragments of love, carefully spilled.
In each embrace, they intertwine,
Painting a world where souls align.

So let them sculpt with every chance,
In quiet rhythm, hearts will dance.
Crafted caresses, fleeting bliss,
In every moment, find a kiss.

Unspoken Paths

In shadows deep, we wander slow,
Where whispered dreams begin to flow.
Silent steps on hidden trails,
Tread softly where the heart unveils.

Each choice we make, a chance to steer,
A journey crafted far from fear.
With every turn, the soul's embrace,
We seek the warmth, the sacred space.

Beneath the stars, our secrets bind,
Paths entwined, our hearts aligned.
In every breath, a story spun,
The quiet paths where love begun.

Through time and space, we stow away,
Each moment locked, yet free to sway.
In unspoken ways, we learn to dance,
Together caught in sacred chance.

As dawn arrives, the world ignites,
With unfulfilled and fierce delights.
The paths we choose, though seldom shown,
With every step, we find our own.

Veils of Vulnerability

Behind the masks, our truths reside,
In tender fears, we dare confide.
Fragile whispers, held so dear,
In veils of trust, we draw you near.

With every tear, the heart takes flight,
In vulnerability, we find our light.
Shadows dance on fragile skin,
A testament to strength within.

Each scar we bear tells tales of grace,
In the depths, we find our place.
A quiet strength, a gentle plea,
To be seen whole, authentically.

Beneath the surface, a storm may brew,
Yet in the calm, we start anew.
In whispered truths, we come alive,
In vulnerability, we thrive.

With every bond that we create,
We navigate the depths of fate.
In every heartbeat, a sacred call,
To embrace our flaws, to stand tall.

The Light Between Us

In quiet moments, our gazes meet,
A spark ignites, both soft and sweet.
The universe spins in stillness true,
Illuminated by the light in you.

Through tangled thoughts, we share our dreams,
In gentle laughter, love redeems.
Our spirits dance, a sacred fire,
With every glance, we lift each other higher.

In every heartbeat, rhythms play,
A melody that guides our way.
The warmth we share, a timeless glow,
A beacon shining, ever so slow.

With every breath, the world unwinds,
In the light, a solace finds.
An unbroken bond, a cosmic thread,
In the light between us, love is spread.

Together we weave the dreams we chase,
In harmony, we find our place.
With every moment, our souls convene,
In the light between us, love unseen.

Pulses and Patterns

In rhythmic beats, our lives entwine,
A tapestry of hearts that shine.
With every pulse, a story told,
In patterns rich, both young and old.

The echoes of the past remind,
In every thread, a bond we find.
A dance of time, a fleeting glance,
In swirls of fate, we find our chance.

Each heartbeat maps the path we tread,
In silent whispers, dreams are bred.
With every rise and fall, we learn,
The flames of love, forever burn.

In every moment, let us embrace,
The pulses that mark our sacred space.
Patterns formed in light and shade,
In this grand dance, love won't fade.

Together we flow, this rhythmic song,
In unity, we both belong.
With every breath, our spirits sing,
In pulses and patterns, joy we bring.

Glimmers of Hope in Data Streams

In lines of code, we find our way,
Fragments of light in the grey.
Silicon dreams whisper and sigh,
In every pulse, the hopes fly high.

Connection blooms where signals meet,
A dance of voices, soft and sweet.
Through bits and bytes, we weave a thread,
A tapestry of words unsaid.

Each surge ignites a spark anew,
From silent depths, the messages brew.
A world of data, vast and wide,
Where human hearts can still reside.

With every click, a journey starts,
Navigating through the floating parts.
Glimmers of hope in every stream,
Together, we unite and dream.

So, let us soar, hand in hand,
In this digital, endless land.
For through the darkness, we will find,
The light of hope, forever kind.

Maps of New Affection

In the quiet corners of our hearts,
Love, like a river, gently starts.
Tracing paths with tender care,
Drawing maps to dreams we share.

With every look, the journey grows,
In whispered words, the feeling flows.
Across the miles, we bridge the gap,
Charting love's unwritten map.

Through laughter bright and tears that fall,
We find our strength, we rise, we call.
In moments shared, the bond does form,
A navigation to the warm.

Explore the landscapes of your soul,
In every dream, we find our whole.
With open hearts, we learn to see,
The beauty in our history.

So let's unfold this gentle chart,
With every beat, we share our heart.
In maps of new affection's grace,
We find our truth in this embrace.

Vibrations in the Void

In silent spaces, vibrations hum,
Echoes of existence softly come.
Resonating through the empty air,
A symphony of souls laid bare.

The universe sings a timeless tune,
Underneath the watchful moon.
Each heartbeat sends a pulse alive,
In the void, we learn to thrive.

Whispers of starlight weave and blend,
Creating worlds that never end.
Through cosmic dance, we intertwine,
In every moment, you are mine.

So draw me close, let spirits meet,
In this embrace, there's no defeat.
For in the void, the silence speaks,
In quiet truths, our journey peaks.

Embrace the sounds that linger near,
In whispered tones, we conquer fear.
Vibrations in the void will guide,
Our hearts aligned, forever bide.

The Essence of Us in the Ether

In the ether where our spirits play,
The essence of us finds its way.
Carving paths in the unseen light,
With every moment, feels so right.

Like shadows dancing in the night,
We merge as one, a wondrous sight.
In every word, in every glance,
Our souls entwined in timeless dance.

The spark of love ignites the air,
As if the universe laid bare.
With gentle whispers, we confess,
The truth of us, in quietness.

Through the layers of time and space,
We explore the depths, we find our place.
In the stillness, our spirits soar,
In the ether's arms, forevermore.

So hold me close, let the journey start,
With every beat, you have my heart.
The essence of us, a radiant thread,
In the ether, our love is spread.

Echoes in the Space Between

Whispers in the silent air,
Fleeting thoughts that drift and share.
Stars twinkle with tales untold,
In the night, their secrets unfold.

Time ticks softly, moments blend,
In the void, where feelings mend.
Hearts are tethered at a glance,
Even when we miss the chance.

Shadows dance in twilight's glow,
Memories like rivers flow.
Every heartbeat, every sigh,
An echo in the endless sky.

Between the worlds, our spirits glide,
Finding peace where dreams abide.
In the hush, we find our way,
Navigating night and day.

Yet in stillness, bonds we weave,
With every thought we believe.
Connected in this vast expanse,
Echoes singing, hearts in trance.

Resilient Bonds in Binary

In the code, our hearts align,
Strings of data intertwine.
Zeros, ones, a dance divine,
In the cloud, our spirits shine.

Through the screens, we build our ties,
Virtual worlds, where friendship lies.
Sharing laughter, sharing tears,
Resilient bonds that last for years.

Every message, every beep,
In this space, our secrets keep.
Threads of hope, we knit with care,
Linking souls in silent prayer.

Binary dreams, together cast,
In this realm, our shadows vast.
Hand in hand, though miles apart,
Resilient ties that warm the heart.

Logic flows, connection strong,
In this world, where we belong.
Through the pixels, love we find,
In every byte, our souls aligned.

Soft Silhouettes of Connection

In twilight's glow, we softly stand,
Silhouettes, hand in hand.
Fleeting dreams like whispers sway,
In the dusk, we find our way.

Beneath the stars, our shadows play,
Hidden words we dare not say.
In the hush of evening's peace,
Bonded souls that never cease.

Every heartbeat is a link,
In the silence, time will shrink.
Gentle moments, soft embrace,
In this space, we find our place.

Each glance speaks a thousand lines,
In the quiet, love defines.
Soft silhouettes, together gleam,
In the night, we share a dream.

Through the dark, we drift and sway,
In the silence, come what may.
Together still, in shadows cast,
In soft silhouettes, we hold fast.

Together Apart

Though miles may stretch, we stand as one,
Beneath the same vast azure sun.
Waves of laughter, tides of grace,
Together apart, we find our place.

Time and distance, they cannot sever,
The ties that bind us, now and forever.
In every sunrise, in every night,
Together apart, we hold the light.

Moments cherished, though far away,
In our hearts, they always stay.
Every message, every sound,
Together apart, our love is found.

Memories linger, sweet and bright,
In the echoes of shared delight.
Though separate paths, we choose to tread,
Together apart, love's thread is spread.

In the stillness, we feel the spark,
Binding us in the endless dark.
Together apart, we are not alone,
In every beat, our love has grown.

A Symphony of Solace

In the quiet of the night,
Soft whispers reach the heart.
Gentle notes take flight,
Weaving peace, a soothing art.

Moonlight dances on the stream,
Reflecting dreams of old.
A melody, a tender beam,
In the stillness, stories told.

Each star a note in the sky,
Composing tales of love.
Songs of hope that never die,
Lifted by the wind above.

Harmony in shadows deep,
Filling spaces left behind.
Eternal promises we keep,
In the silence, solace binds.

So let the music flow,
In every heart it finds,
A symphony to grow,
In the beauty of our minds.

The Space Between

Between the breaths we share,
Lies a world of dreams untold.
Moments linger in the air,
Soft and delicate, like gold.

A glance, a smile, a touch,
Echoes of what lies ahead.
Fleeting seconds mean so much,
In the silence, words are said.

This gap, a canvas wide,
With colors of our becoming.
In the stillness, we confide,
Listening to the heartbeat's drumming.

Each heartbeat tells a tale,
Woven in this sacred space.
In love, we shall not fail,
For here, we find our place.

So let us dwell, my dear,
Within this hallowed scene.
In the space, we'll persevere,
Together, through the unseen.

Unraveled Threads

In the tapestry of time,
Threads of fate intertwine.
Weaving stories, sublime,
In the fabric, we define.

Colors fade, yet still we see,
Patterns of a life once known.
Each strand whispers, 'Come to me,'
In the quiet, seeds are sown.

Unraveled threads, a scatter,
Life's complexities unfold.
Amidst the silence, what matters
Is the warmth of hearts, and bold.

We gather pieces, bit by bit,
Stitching love with every tear.
Finding beauty where we sit,
In each unraveling share.

So let the needle guide our way,
Through the patterns, and the knots.
In the mess, we find our play,
In the chaos, love connects the dots.

Vibrations of Belonging

In the heartbeat of the night,
Whispers of the soul unite.
We find strength in shared delight,
Vibrations of belonging, bright.

A circle drawn, where smiles gleam,
Connected by the threads of hope.
In laughter's warm and gentle beam,
We discover how to cope.

Beyond the distances we chart,
The echoes of affection swell.
In every pause, in every start,
A resonance we know so well.

Together, we embrace the call,
In moments vast and small.
In unity, we rise, we fall,
A symphony, we give our all.

So let the rhythm weave us tight,
In this dance of hearts, we find.
Vibrations hold us through the night,
In belonging, we are kind.

Interwoven Tails of Time

In shadows long, we weave our tales,
Across the years, where memory pales.
Threads of laughter, threads of tears,
Intertwined, they calm our fears.

Moments caught in silken dreams,
Flowing rivers, quiet streams.
Time's embrace, a gentle hold,
Stories whispered, truths retold.

As seasons turn, as petals fall,
We gather strength, we stand tall.
Together through the ebb and flow,
In every heart, our legacies grow.

Stars remind us of our grace,
In the void, we find our place.
With every breath, a new refrain,
The tapestry, a sacred gain.

Eternal threads, so soft, entwined,
Binding lives, forever aligned.
In the fabric of what we find,
We cherish our interconnected mind.

Fragments of Glass

Scattered shards, a broken past,
Reflecting light, so bright, so vast.
Each fragment holds a secret deep,
In colors lost, our stories seep.

The glimmer draws our hearts in close,
A fragile beauty we can't oppose.
In every piece, a tale to share,
Concealed within, we learn to care.

With tender hands, we piece and mend,
From shattered hopes, new paths we send.
In the chaos, clarity shines,
A mosaic built from faded lines.

Through shattered glass, we see it clear,
Our wounds may heal, our hearts endear.
In jagged edges, light can play,
Transforming night into the day.

The beauty of the fragmented whole,
Each broken part, a healing soul.
In every glimmer, we find our way,
From shards of glass, we paint the day.

Fragments of Us

In whispered dreams, we softly sway,
Echoes of love that will not stray.
Pieces scattered, yet we remain,
Together bound through joy and pain.

Each moment shared, a puzzle made,
In the light of dawn, our fears do fade.
From laughter's peak to sorrow's gloom,
In each fragment, we find our bloom.

The memories stitched in twilight's grace,
Reflections show our tangled embrace.
Through vibrant hues, our journey glows,
In every tear, a beauty shows.

As seasons shift, our roots run deep,
In every promise, love we keep.
Fragments of us, both whole and torn,
In our hearts, a light is born.

Together, we dance on time's soft thread,
Woven stories where love has led.
Each fragment holds a piece of trust,
For in it all, lies the heart of us.

Sentiments in Suspended Reality

In whispered hues, the moments blend,
Reality bends, and time suspends.
Thoughts like feathers in the air,
Lifted softly, light as prayer.

Caught between the now and dream,
Ideas flow like a gentle stream.
Emotions dance on silver threads,
In twilight's glow, where spirit treads.

The echoes of our silent pleas,
Carried on the evening breeze.
Each heartbeat syncs with realms untold,
In this stillness, we are bold.

Through layers deep, our truths arise,
In muted shades, beneath the skies.
The world outside may fade away,
Within this space, we choose to stay.

Suspended here, where feelings soar,
We find the peace we all adore.
In fleeting moments, bold and bright,
Sentiments woven, pure delight.

The Art of Digital Tenderness

Fingers dance on glowing screens,
Crafting love in pixel scenes.
Words woven with a gentle grace,
Across the void, we find our place.

In every tap, a heartbeat shared,
In silence held, our souls are bared.
Emojis smile, as feelings flow,
In virtual realms, our passions glow.

Moments captured, snapshots flee,
Framed in time, you and me.
With every click, a bond we weave,
Digital threads that we believe.

Through glimmers bright and shadows cast,
In every message, gardens grow fast.
With every share, our joys combine,
The art of tenderness, divine.

In this space, kindness reigns supreme,
A tapestry stitched from our dreams.
Through screens we reach, our hearts align,
In this soft glow, your hand in mine.

Bonded by Algorithms

In shadows cast by screens we dwell,
Where logic sings, and numbers tell.
We search for truth in coded streams,
In binary worlds, we weave our dreams.

Across the wires, a pulse ignites,
Connected hearts in digital nights.
Each click a bond, each swipe a thread,
In this new realm, our past is shed.

The data flows like rivers wide,
In virtual realms, from you, I can't hide.
A tapestry of ones and zeros,
In silent echoes, I find my heroes.

But in this matrix, do we feel?
Or just reflect what we conceal?
With every message, a piece we share,
In ones and zeros, do we dare?

Yet still there’s warmth in coded space,
A fleeting touch in cyberspace.
Together we dance through the electric haze,
Bound by algorithms in a digital maze.

Pulses Through the Network

A flicker here, a blink there too,
Electric whispers, connecting me and you.
In vibrant threads, our voices blend,
Pulses through the network that never end.

Bytes of laughter, joy coded bright,
Frequencies echoing through the night.
A touch of love in the circuits deep,
Awake in dreams while the world's asleep.

The screens glow warm like starlit skies,
In every heart, a truth that lies.
Rhythms beating in digital pride,
Together we stand, though worlds divide.

Patterns emerge in the tangled mesh,
A dance of spirits, our souls enmesh.
Pulses through wires, a lively spree,
Boundless freedom, you and me.

In the void, we search for more,
Each connection opens a door.
Through pixels bright, our spirits fly,
Under the electronic sky.

The Glistening Surface of Longing

Beneath the glow of artificial light,
A shimmer dances, haunting the night.
Reflections of dreams in a window's pane,
The glistening surface conceals the pain.

Yearning whispers through the screen,
A silent pulse where we have been.
In fleeting glances, our hearts may race,
Yet solitude lingers in this space.

Voices echo in the void so deep,
A haunting melody that won't let me sleep.
Caught in the web of hopes unspoken,
In each lost signal, a promise broken.

Yet in this gleam, I find my way,
Through shadows that stretch, chasing the day.
Longing glimmers, a fragile thread,
Binding us close, though worlds are spread.

In every heartbeat, I sense the call,
The glistening surface, our rise and fall.
Through longing's haze, we grasp and reach,
A silent lesson life will teach.

Cloaked in Connectivity

Wrapped in signals, we drift and sway,
Cloaked in connectivity, we find our way.
Through digital currents, we start to blend,
In every heartbeat, a message we send.

Across the distance, our spirits meet,
Tangled webs beneath our feet.
In every login, a tale unfolds,
In virtual arms, the lonely hold.

The world spins on, a screen-lit space,
Cloaked in dreams that we chase.
A symphony of clicks in the night,
Guiding the lost to the light.

Yet shadows linger, a haunting chill,
In endless scrolling, a silent thrill.
We seek connection, yet fear the sight,
Of genuine warmth amid the fright.

In every heartbeat, a story lies,
Cloaked in masks, we wear our lies.
Yet in the dark, a spark will glow,
In connectivity, our true selves show.

Dances of the Disembodied

Whispers float on fragile air,
Echoes of souls in silent dance.
Flickering lights, shadows dare,
Threads of dreams in a timeless trance.

Barefoot on the edge of night,
They swirl like smoke in fleeting sight.
A rhythm woven, soft and light,
In the dark, they find their flight.

Spirits twine in a tender sway,
Among the stars, they lose their way.
In this realm where lost hearts play,
Each step forgotten, yet they stay.

Voices rise in a ghostly choir,
A symphony of lost desire.
In silent woos, they lift us higher,
Then fade away, as dreams conspire.

So dance, dear heart, in ether's light,
Find freedom in the deepest night.
In every turn, a glimpse of flight,
In every breath, a soft goodbye.

Bridges of Understanding

Two hearts crossed on paths untold,
In the silence, stories unfold.
Lines of fate, both warm and cold,
Building bridges, brave and bold.

Words exchanged, a gentle flow,
In shared laughter, seeds they sow.
Through the tempest, love will grow,
Together now, they're never slow.

Hands held tight in darkest days,
Guiding souls through life's maze.
In every challenge, hope displays,
A beacon bright that always stays.

Eyes that meet without a sound,
In deep understanding, love is found.
Through storms of life, forever bound,
In unity, their hearts resound.

So let us walk this winding road,
With open hearts and gentle code.
In every step, our stories load,
On bridges built, love's pure abode.

The Space Between the Codes

In the realm of binary dreams,
Where silence hums and wisdom beams.
The space between is not as it seems,
A canvas where the heart redeems.

Within each pulse, a hidden spark,
Binary whispers in the dark.
The silent codes leave their mark,
Creating light from muted arc.

In coded lines, emotions weave,
Patterns forming what we perceive.
In algorithms, love can cleave,
Through every signal, we believe.

The gaps define what’s meant to be,
In absence lies our synergy.
From whispered signals, we are free,
In every pause, truth's melody.

So let us linger in this space,
Between the codes, we find our grace.
In quiet moments, we embrace,
The harmony of time and place.

Portraits of Shared Silence

In stillness, we find our glow,
Painted words in whispers flow.
A canvas brushed with hues unknown,
In silence, our true selves shown.

Each moment speaks without a sound,
In stillness, connections are found.
Hearts beat softly, tightly wound,
In shared silence, love unbound.

Eyes exchange what words can't share,
In quietude, a bond laid bare.
Through every silence, we declare,
The depth of feelings, laying spare.

Captured frames of tender thought,
In the quiet, battles fought.
With every pause, we learn what’s sought,
In shared silence, love is caught.

So let us linger in this space,
Where portraits form without a trace.
In shared silence, find our place,
In every heartbeat, love’s embrace.

Dreams in the Feedback Loop

In whispers soft, the echoes play,
Through time and space, they find their way.
Illusions dance in shadows bright,
Awake, we drift, in endless night.

Pixels shimmer, stories unfold,
As visions blur, our hearts grow bold.
Time bends here in this looping maze,
In dreams, we linger, lost in haze.

Chasing trails of fading light,
Our wishes born from silent flight.
In circuits crossed, the worlds align,
Beyond the real, your hand in mine.

Reflections twist in motion's grip,
A cycle spun, the heart's sweet trip.
In every turn, a chance to mend,
In tech's embrace, we never end.

So let us dwell where dreams concuss,
In feedback's flow, it's just us.
Awake or sleep, the tale is told,
In whispers soft, we dare be bold.

Embracing the Ether

In currents deep where silence lies,
We float between the stars and sighs.
The ether sings a tune so pure,
In its embrace, our hearts endure.

Connected souls, though far apart,
In every beat, we share one heart.
Through wires and waves, we start to feel,
The pulse of love, electric, real.

Words ignite in vibrant streams,
In dreams, we weave our shared extremes.
Every message, a bridge we build,
In unseen realms, our hopes fulfilled.

The universe, a vast expanse,
In cosmic waves, we take our chance.
With open hearts, we dance on air,
In ether's grasp, we find our care.

So let us soar on whispers light,
Embraced by stars, through endless night.
In every breath, our spirits fuse,
In ether's warmth, we cannot lose.

Virtual Threads of Affection

In lines so fine, our feelings thread,
Across the screen, where dreams are spread.
With every click, a bond we form,
In virtual realms, we find our norm.

Emojis spill like painted hearts,
Across the miles, we play our parts.
A hug, a smile, a wink, a sigh,
In coded love, we learn to fly.

The distance fades with every post,
In shared moments, we feel the most.
Through photos shared and stories spun,
In every pixel, we become one.

Threads weave tight, though miles apart,
With every message, we share our art.
In bytes and bits, emotions swirl,
In cyberspace, we dance and twirl.

So let our voices rise and blend,
In this vast web, there is no end.
In virtual threads, we find affection,
A tapestry of deep connection.

The Touch of Pixels

A gentle swipe, a world awakes,
In colors bright, the silence breaks.
With every touch, a spark ignites,
In soft-lit screens, two hearts take flight.

The canvas glows, imagination flows,
In pixel dreams, the feeling grows.
Through every frame, we learn to see,
The art of love, you and me.

We stitch our lives in vibrant hues,
With every click, we craft our views.
In digital space, emotions blend,
With every byte, our souls transcends.

Your laughter fills the empty space,
In touch of pixels, we find grace.
The warmth of screens like sunlit days,
In every glance, our hearts ablaze.

So let us celebrate this dance,
In pixels bright, we find romance.
In every color, a world reborn,
In joyous touch, our love adorned.

Chasing Shadows of Togetherness

In twilight's glow, we softly roam,
Finding solace, we call this home.
Hands intertwined, our hearts take flight,
Chasing shadows, embracing the night.

Whispers of dreams dance in the air,
In this moment, nothing can compare.
Shared laughter brightens the fading day,
Together we weave, come what may.

Across the fields where wildflowers sway,
Your eyes reflect the last light's play.
In silence, we share an unbroken vow,
Together forever, here and now.

When stars ignite the darkened skies,
I see our future in your eyes.
No distance can dim our radiant flame,
In the chase of shadows, love's our name.

With every heartbeat, we feel alive,
In this dance of shadows, we strive.
Chasing moments, forever entwined,
In togetherness, our love defined.

Lyrical Pixels

In the digital realm, colors collide,
Where every pixel tells stories wide.
Crafting emotions with every hue,
Lyrical magic, forever anew.

Vibrant shades twirl in rhythmic grace,
Each click, each tap, a heartfelt embrace.
From chaos emerges a symphonic view,
In this canvas, our dreams come true.

Brushstrokes of laughter paint the sky,
With every beat, our spirits fly.
Captured moments, so vivid and clear,
In lyrical pixels, I hold you near.

Fragments of life, we gather and weave,
Stitched together in what we believe.
Digital whispers in a timeless song,
Through lyrical pixels, where we belong.

In every snapshot, a heartbeat remains,
A symphony played in love's refrains.
Together we journey, through this delight,
Creating our world, pixel-perfect light.

Spheres of Sensation

Within the spheres of fleeting time,
Every heartbeat dances, pure and prime.
Textures of moments, we softly embrace,
In gentle whispers, we find our place.

The touch of the breeze, a soft caress,
Filling our spirits, banishing stress.
Colors expand in a vivid array,
Spheres of sensation carry us away.

With every glance, a world unfolds,
Magic swirls as the future holds.
Awakening senses, one by one,
In this vast expanse, we find the sun.

The rhythm of life beats strong and true,
In the play of sensations, I sense you.
Each moment cherished, a timeless glow,
Within these spheres, our love will grow.

Guided by feelings that intertwine,
In this grand journey, our hearts align.
Through spheres of sensation, we will glide,
In harmony's melody, side by side.

Kaleidoscope of Connections

In a kaleidoscope, colors combine,
A fusion of souls, your hand in mine.
Reflecting moments, bright and bold,
In connections vibrant, stories unfold.

With every turn, a new path appears,
Weaving together laughter and tears.
Infinite patterns, ever in motion,
Kaleidoscope dreams stir deep emotion.

Fractals of heartbeats, dancing in light,
Illuminating shadows, banishing night.
Through shifting angles, we dive below,
In this tapestry, love's patterns grow.

Each connection whispers secrets untold,
In the warmth of presence, we break the cold.
Colors intertwine, creating our song,
In this kaleidoscope, where we belong.

As the world spins, we hold on tight,
Finding solace in the shared delight.
With every turn, our spirits align,
In the kaleidoscope of hearts, we shine.

Colors of Shared Dreams

In twilight's arms, our visions blend,
A canvas rich, where hopes transcend.
Each hue a whisper, soft and bright,
Together we chase the fading light.

With every stroke, our hearts align,
In shades of laughter, joy divine.
A palette wide, we dare to see,
The colors of our unity.

Through storms and sunshine, we will paint,
A masterpiece, both wild and quaint.
In every shade, our truths reside,
In colors bold, we will abide.

In starlit skies, our dreams unfurl,
As hopes ignite and sweetly swirl.
With every moment, we ignite,
A spectrum born of love's delight.

So let us color the world anew,
In every dream, there's me and you.
Together, hand in hand we strive,
In vibrant bonds, we come alive.

Breath Between the Words

In silence rests the stirring truth,
A pause that forms a bridge of youth.
Between each phrase, a heartbeat waits,
Whispering through the heavy gates.

The air is thick with unspoken dreams,
In shadows cast by sunlight beams.
A space where feelings take their flight,
And souls collide in purest light.

With every sigh, a story spins,
In breathless moments, life begins.
An echo dances in the air,
As thoughts entwine, a sacred prayer.

In tender gaps where silence breathes,
Our hearts unearth what love believes.
A soft exchange, as spirits meld,
In breaths between, our truths compelled.

Each word a step, each pause a sign,
In melodies of the divine.
Through breaths we form a bond so rare,
In whispered notes, we show we care.

An Odyssey of Togetherness

On windswept shores, we sail as one,
With maps of dreams, adventures spun.
Through ocean's roar and starry skies,
We weave our tales in love's reprise.

Each wave we ride brings us much closer,
In every heartbeat, life's exposure.
With every challenge, hand in hand,
An odyssey across the land.

The tides may shift, the storms may call,
Yet in our hearts, we shall not fall.
With courage strong and spirits free,
Together, we find our destiny.

Through mountains high and valleys low,
In every turn, our love will grow.
With every dawn, a chance to mend,
An endless journey with no end.

In echoes of laughter, we thrive,
For in togetherness, we come alive.
A bond unbroken, true and bold,
An odyssey that must be told.

Shapes of Longing

In shadows deep, my heart unfolds,
A thousand shapes, in silence told.
Each curve a memory, every line,
A trace of love, forever mine.

With every angle, every shade,
A longing born, in time delayed.
An artful design, both sharp and sweet,
In every glance, our souls entreat.

The contours of our unclaimed dreams,
In whispered sighs, the longing streams.
Through valleys vast and hills we climb,
We seek the forms of love divine.

In shapes of yearning, we collide,
With every contour, hearts open wide.
In spaces filled with soft despair,
We craft our hopes with gentle care.

So let us mold these shapes anew,
In every heartbeat, me and you.
For in the longing, we define,
The art of love, eternally entwined.

Translucent Trust

In shadows soft, we find the light,
A whisper shared, a gentle fight.
Through fragile bonds, hearts intertwine,
A trust that glows, forever shine.

With eyes that see beyond the veil,
Our laughter echoes, never pale.
In moments lost, we rise anew,
Translucent dreams, in shades of blue.

Through storms of doubt, we hold our ground,
In unity, our strength is found.
With each soft breath, a promise made,
In lucid trust, we'll never fade.

In silence deep, our spirits dance,
A sacred space, a tender glance.
With every step, we pave the way,
A path where love will always stay.

Through time and space, our stories blend,
In trust reborn, we transcend.
Together bound, we forge our fate,
In translucent light, we resonate.

Celestial Conversations

Beneath the stars, whispers unfold,
In celestial realms, secrets told.
With every glance toward the sky,
We weave our dreams where comets fly.

The moonlight hums a gentle tune,
In cosmic flow, hearts become strewn.
Stars dance around in endless waltz,
With each heartbeat, love's gravitation halts.

Galaxies spin in silent grace,
Unveiling truths in time and space.
In every twinkle, souls relay,
The promises of night and day.

Nebulas swirl, colors collide,
In vibrant hues, our fates abide.
Through cosmic tides, we share our fears,
In conversations void of tears.

As dawn draws near, the sky awakes,
With whispered hopes that love remakes.
In celestial dreams, we'll reside,
Bound together, forever tied.

Eros in Electric Dreams

In neon glows, our shadows merge,
With every spark, we feel the surge.
Electric pulses, hearts align,
In wicked whims, our souls entwine.

Through circuits wild, our passions race,
A rhythm found in cyberspace.
In whispered bytes, desires soar,
As Eros reigns through every door.

In flickering lights, our spirits play,
Creating worlds where we can stay.
Through tangled paths, we dare to tread,
In electric dreams, love’s flame is bred.

With every touch, a current flows,
In pixelated highs and lows.
Together bright, we spark and ignite,
In shadows lost, we find our light.

As dawn breaks in, the dream might fade,
But in our hearts, the bond won’t jade.
In electric whispers, we'll believe,
In Eros’ arms, we’ll never leave.

Finding Warmth in Circuits

In tangled wires, our hearts connect,
In digital warmth, we find respect.
With every click, a spark ignites,
In circuits woven, love ignites.

Through screens we laugh, through pixels cry,
In every stroke, our spirits fly.
A warmth that pulses, steady beat,
In electric fields, our souls meet.

With codes of love, we build our dream,
In every byte, we find our theme.
Together wrapped in soft embrace,
In circuits wide, we find our place.

As signals hum through every wire,
In harmony, we lift and inspire.
Through storms and glitches, we will thrive,
In warmth of circuits, we’re alive.

With every wave, our spirits meld,
In glowing lights, our longing held.
Finding warmth where hearts convene,
In circuits rich, a timeless sheen.

Garden of Shared Moments

In the quiet corners, blooms unfold,
Laughter dances in the shade of gold.
Hands entwined, stories softly told,
In this garden, warmth and memories hold.

Petals brush against the gentle breeze,
Echoes of joy, whispers that tease.
Each shared moment, a treasure to seize,
In this haven, hearts find their ease.

Sunlight kisses the dew-kissed ground,
In every heartbeat, love is found.
Nature's rhythm, a sweet surround,
In this space, pure bliss is crowned.

Evening descends, stars take their flight,
Under the moon, our dreams ignite.
In the garden, everything feels right,
Together forever, souls in the light.

With every season, the petals change,
Yet our bond remains, never strange.
In this garden, we'll always arrange,
New moments bloom, through joy or grange.

Resonance of Souls.

In the stillness, hearts start to sing,
A melody formed, a beautiful thing.
Echoes of laughter, the joy they bring,
In the dance of the night, our spirits take wing.

Through valleys deep and mountains high,
We find our paths, as stars align in the sky.
The whispers of kinship, never to die,
In the resonance of souls, we learn to fly.

Every story woven, like threads of old,
In the tapestry of life, our truths unfold.
Together we stand, and never be sold,
For the warmth of connection is priceless gold.

As seasons change and years drift by,
The bond we share will never say goodbye.
Through laughter and tears, under wide-open sky,
In the resonance of souls, love can't deny.

In the pulse of the world, we find our way,
Together we rise with each coming day.
With hearts intertwined, come what may,
In the resonance of souls, forever we stay.

Whispers in the Digital Fog

Beneath the glow of screens that shine,
Connections forged, a new design.
In virtual realms, our hearts align,
Whispers travel, timeless and divine.

Amidst the noise, a gentle call,
Emojis speak where silence falls.
In every message, a tale enthralls,
In the digital fog, love conquers all.

Moments captured, pixels collide,
In data streams, we take our ride.
Sharing dreams in this vast tide,
Through wires and waves, our hearts abide.

Time seems to blur as we log in,
In this space, new friendships begin.
Through whispers of hope, laughter, and sin,
In the digital fog, we all fit in.

Yet in the distance, we crave the real,
A hand to hold, a heart to feel.
Still, in this realm, connections heal,
In whispers of light, our truths reveal.

Heartbeats of the Connected

In the pulse of existence, rhythms intertwine,
Across the miles, a love so divine.
Linked by our hearts, in sync every sign,
Together we thrive, your heartbeat is mine.

Through trials and joys, we stand hand in hand,
In this dance of life, we make our stand.
Moments of silence, perfectly planned,
In the heartbeats of connected, we understand.

With each gentle thump, our stories are spun,
In laughter and tears, two souls become one.
Through shadows and light, our journey's begun,
In the heartbeats of connected, we've already won.

Echoes of love in the silent night,
In every shared glance, our spirits take flight.
With hope in our hearts, we shine ever bright,
In the heartbeats of connected, everything's right.

Together we rise, as the world spins around,
In every heartbeat, our joy can be found.
Through ebb and flow, in love we are bound,
In the heartbeats of connected, forever profound.

Printed in the USA
CPSIA information can be obtained
at www.ICGtesting.com
LVHW021958231024
794641LV00008B/112

9 789916 891551